PRAISE FOR Cat's Tongue

"There is so much to admire in Cat's Tongue: the rich language, the surprising images, the fraught figurative landscapes, etc. Perhaps more than anything, though, these are poems that reach for the unexpected human moments—the moments that remind us we're alive—the moments that, ultimately, make a life."

—MICHAEL SHEWMAKER, AUTHOR OF *PENUMBRA*

"In Kathleen Winter's new collection *Cat's Tongue*, memory is a thing to encounter untamed, to be rediscovered and confronted before it's lost again. These poems 'go backwards / in experience, subtracting yes from yes' as they unearth secrets and regrets and yearnings, as they reckon the past with the present. Through the glint and gloom of memory, these poems portray the self in all its strength and grief, all with Winter's trademark keenness and lyrical grace."

—W. TODD KANEKO, AUTHOR OF *THIS IS HOW THE BONE SING*

"A book of fragmented memories, of mysteries. And, yes, a book to remember for its amazing lines:

> Memory! I send the last dog to greet you / with his one wild eye //
> Is courage biochemical, / a genetic inheritance? //
> How many times have I tripped, laid flat by / the trap of a fast-firing mind?//
> Why rise from bed / when the owl yet sings in the mesquite / and no one has
> made coffee. . . .

And this is only a sample of Kathleen Winter's wondrous book. Read it, savor it!"

—SUSAN TERRIS, AUTHOR OF *FAMILIAR TENSE*

The TRP Chapbook Series

SERIES EDITOR: J. BRUCE FULLER

THE TRP CHAPBOOK SERIES highlights work by emerging authors who have not yet released their first full-length book in addition to established authors working on shorter projects.

BOOKS IN THIS SERIES:

Jose Hernandez Diaz, *The Fire Eater*

Kara Krewer, *Born-Again Anything*

Richard Boada, *We Find Each Other in the Darkness*

James Jabar, *Whatever Happened to Black Boys?*

Ryan Vine, *WARD*

Kathleen Winter, *Cat's Tongue*

Cat's Tongue

poems

KATHLEEN WINTER

★trp

THE UNIVERSITY PRESS OF SHSU
HUNTSVILLE, TEXAS

Printed in the United States of America
Published by Texas Review Press Huntsville, Texas 77341
Library of Congress Cataloging-in-Publication Data
Names: Winter, Kathleen.
Title: Cat's tongue : poems / Kathleen Winter.
Other titles: TRP chapbook series.
Description: Huntsville, Texas : Texas Review Press, [2022]
Series: The TRP chapbook series |
Identifiers: LCCN 2021044578 (print) | LCCN 2021044579 (ebook)ISBN
9781680032697 (paperback) | ISBN 9781680032703 (ebook)
Subjects: LCSH: Texas–Poetry. | LCGFT: Poetry.
Classification: LCC PS3623.I6724 C38 2022 (print)
LCC PS3623.I6724 (ebook) | DDC 811/.6–dc23
LC record available at https://lccn.loc.gov/2021044578
LC ebook record available at https://lccn.loc.gov/2021044579
Cover photo courtesy of girl-with-red-hat@unsplash
Cover & Book Design: PJ Carlisle

for Don Bogen

Contents

We were not that far from what had been
given us to call home.

—MAGDALENA ZURAWSKI

Beside Myself

This is temporary   a misunderstanding
between myself and me.

How I came to be caught in my own net,
the red blur of an old girl.

Half-submerged body—craft to carry just one animal.

I pull myself up
by the boot-strap of my braid.

Memory! I send the last dog to greet you
with his one wild eye.

Some days I want certainty, some days, revelation.

I'm thinking of instances
when how something felt was not what I expected,
like the time a naturalist brought a snake to Cambridge
Elementary. Gathered in a carpeted common
space outside our classrooms, we sat on the floor, waiting
for the snake to make the rounds, passed hand to
hand among us. Not slippery, not cool, but heavy
with inertia, the reptile was a sleek celebrity,
days away from hunger.

Days away from hunger,
the reptile was a sleek celebrity, inert and heavy,
not cool, not slippery, passed hand to hand
among us. Waiting around for the snake outside
our classrooms, we sat on the floor's carpeted
common space, gathered. Cambridge Elementary
brought in a snake, a naturalist. I'm not thinking of
how time *was,* but of what the instance felt like . . .
of something I expected.

Force of Habit

The woman in the Oldsmobile was awfully young
to have a kid her kid would have said if she'd had
a voice, not just a body jittery inside her precious cotton
dress with ducks stitched in the smocked bodice
flat across her washboard chest. A woman's hand
was every bit as flat when she had to slap somebody's
face. It wasn't best sometimes to have a voice in case
you asked the woman one too many times how Seguin
was different from Saigon or where the dad had
gone or who was gonna fix the swing or when can we
get a collie or what's wrong with twirling a lock
of hair around your finger all day long it felt
so smooth & cool around your index finger &
released & caught & wound again, secured.
What's wrong with messing with this living little
bit of you, a darling little thing. You couldn't stop it
even if you wanted to.

A Green Golf Shirt with Holes

Out of nowhere
grief, burning sting

sunscreen in both eyes.

Will it ever stop?
You gave me something

is it a taste

love, this bitter preservative?
Worn soft

by the decades you favored it

the shirt hangs to my thighs
a shield that couldn't save you.

Savor this slow drip

medicinal salt-slurry
in my mouth, my breath

—together we saw it—

then with just one hand
you made the alligator disappear.

The Twins

If I had a cast and children wrote on it
what was it that I broke?
If I had a dachshund in the hospital
with cotton skin and nurses wrote on it
what was it that they wrote?
That year we all were animals:
Hallie a goat, Mary a gerbil, I was
a toad. We slipped each other notes
painstakingly enhanced with colored pencil.
What we knew was euchre, coffee-
milk, rainbow caster sugar, the ferns
their mother painted on a white silk
dress as it lay across her four-poster.
Did the twins really brush their hair
a hundred times after dinner, sleep in
lace-trimmed ankle socks, clean their faces
with that concoction made by a Hungarian
with a hyphenated name? The liquid
separated from suspended solids so they
always had to shake it. It came
in rectangular bottles.
For my birthday, in a coffee can, they gave me
this mountain-laurel tree I stowed in
my dry little mind.

How We Understood Waste

With this hose in my hand I think of poets
slain by gardening—Rilke, reportedly by a rose.
It kills me to remember chrysanthemums
some boys gave some girls on days of high school
football games: cabbage-size blossoms that trailed
blue ribbons dangling past the waists
of cheerleaders and drill team members, twirlers
who fixed them to uniforms, puncturing stems
with hatpins topped by oblong plastic pearls.
Like mutant prom corsages engorged
with mindless pride, those white and gold-petaled
poufs of allowance.

How many hatpin stabs would it take me to kill
that me, I wonder as I water these idle dying roses
too entitled to actually flower, persisting only as leaf
beneath the fir trees' shade. And number the oleanders
among my garden's dangers—one with fuchsia petals,
the other blossoming baby pink, with dark green leaves
tapered like 70's fingernails. They can poison a child.
Billions of oleanders line Texas highways that carry
yellow buses full of players to the games, Friday nights
when the air cools enough for young bodies to rush
quick as the old ones drink. After school we ate
white bread spread with butter and sprinkled
with sugar—we were ten-year-olds, but seven years later.
For us, *waste* was just another misspelled word.

In Karnes County,

sure, it's a fine thing to get in communication with a fault. I'm good at looking for faults—maybe I should be a geologist. But I'd rather find iguanodon bones than oil or gas, rather find water. I knew a diviner's daughter who quit school at sixteen to tour with her punk band, ran into a Swedish man on the train to Hamburg, moved to Spain to live on receipts of his deals, stashed in his mom's house during his seven-year sentence. He looked like a kinder, duller Mick Jagger. He gave her a roll of bills worth thousands to hide in her backpack till they reached Ibiza. I wouldn't call her a gold digger, but she knew where to find water. If you met her parents, you wouldn't fault her. Whenever I visit Kenedy I miss her—the only other girl who left, the one who knew Karnes will be dry forever.

The Writing Teacher as Rampant Stag

Here's my rule: I announce it with swagger. I tell it to students as Someone Who Knows. My rule is an hour. Everyone has an hour, half hour, a page. Don't try to soften it, don't tell me you merit my only exception: an infant. You? With your wellspring of vanity, your sunscreens, your elaborate hand-painted hair? I can guess you'll choose to be fruitless. I, however, have a daughter. Imperious as the elements, I have arguments, points too numerous to number. You hear me outside your somnolence, trampling the morning depthless with blackness, stamping my hooves through your flimsy dream. Furious in thicket, reverberant in woods beyond your walls, thrashing through scrub, colliding with naked burnished madrone I heave myself with my rule through your feeble screens into your untrained ear resistant ear insolent ear your prone ear, recumbent as an inconsolable sofa. Woman, I have a rule.

Incandescence

What wouldn't I give
for some of those drugs
we took so casually in college,
the meth in a closet
during a party, all by myself,
reading *Sons and Lovers*
with a flashlight. Or the meth
in somebody's bathroom
during a party, by myself
reading *The Crying of Lot 49*.
Characters will come alive
with color before your eyes,
crammed into your boyfriend's
hall closet among his jean
jackets and polychrome bathrobe
as gaudy as Joseph's.
They're standing right next
to you, lovely as you are,
green and scared as you are,
over the fence and dying
to cross a field but terrified
about the cows.
When my friend was a wild
fresh NYU grad she married
a stranger and moved to Cairo
to start a family.
There she stands at the top
of a pyramid, wearing flat little
sneakers and houndstooth slacks,
her sly smile.
Is courage biochemical,
a genetic inheritance?
Ignited, it's rocket fuel
that can blast a half-
orphaned immigrant kid
to the stratosphere of sheiks
and U. N. chiefs. Often I wish
to be near it, singe my eyelashes.
Tonight I want to be alone
in good company.

Matchbook Picturing Two Women:

"Beauty & Charm"

T's not for Texas, not for Tennessee.
Not for T-bone or T-strap either.
This T stands for legalese: *traps for the unwary.*
Sometimes the trap's benign as a rhyme scheme
but it could be toxic as the bottle.
Might be a strip tease or sirens' harmonies.
Traps may be dope or T-notes, bitcoin, power
trips or greed: the mousetrap's mouthful
or a quicksand kiss to sink you to your knees.
How many times have I tripped, laid flat by
the trap of a fast-firing mind, Ferris wheel
flattery? It's one deadly T-stop: romance
meets reality. Relic of our rigid-gendered
South, crucify me on your mid-century
mystique—Beauty & Charm
never suited me to a T.

Crazing

Duchamp claimed we love the frescoes for their cracks.
Let's say the same for ceramics.

For voices.

A thin road crosses the Florentine bridge known for gold,
where a girl bought a braided bracelet

that failed decades later, Frost-wise.

Until the last gasp (Wilde's wallpaper)
who can say what will stay.

But small oil portraits may be tucked away,
have a plausible survival rate:

give me an heiress in miniature,
I'll give you a commission.

Make of fragments a down-to-earth value—
Duchamp, calling himself "a breather."

The Breeders struck a similar chord.

Come closer: note the crazing in the glaze.

In the trick space of sleep
I found an earlier version of myself

might not have survived without suffrage.

Duchamp's ex-wife suffered his chess obsession
until one night he found she'd glued

the pieces to the board.
The worst marriages make the best divorces.

Pas de Deux

He seized her,
lifted her up & stumbled
around in two or three complete circles
before he set her back down on her sneakers
beneath the oaks. She remembered this forever or so
far as forever goes for a soul still moving forward bodily
but backward & forward continually mentally like a barely
trained bird dog, retrieving the wrong things as often
as not, not their elevation but the slope beneath
them where he put her down, unstable soil
beside a dead-end driveway, the lot
in front belonging to
another pair.

Cuomo's Important Failures

This moment, this very sensation,
must be what drives people to crime
or at least pornography.
I can almost imagine the state of mind
I want to have, but don't, can't.

In a sleeping bag
on the floor of a dorm room,
hearing, for the first time,
Blue, Joni Mitchell's lyrics
lurid with futurity.
Then Brecht, then the anorexic saints,
the Marxian critics making my parents
so nervous at Christmas.

A welter, a tangle, a bramble of longings
that don't abate in the later decades,
just become marginally more repressible,
slightly easier to bulldoze with focus.

I recall my philosophy professor
reading aloud "Musée des Beaux Arts"
as he tried to seduce me,
his wife and baby at home
in what must have been a too-small apartment.

What lust drove him to approach me—
was it only novelty, or can we finally agree,
across the long years, on tonight's despair?

Cat's Tongue

Finally she saw him again, at a college reunion. Four gaudy chandeliers in the ballroom shivered out splinters of light; the music was southern-fried rock, decades old and sounding worse than ever. In his unbearable thirst she'd given him the last, the first, the only water from the spring of her body—a theatrical gesture only they two could remember. He wore a long-sleeved blue cotton shirt, as he and his brother had worn so often years before. Even the greying hair shone gold above his lupine eyes, which found her through his thin-rimmed, expensive, glasses, through the chattering crowd in between them. She wanted to say something to him, to bite it into the base of his neck deftly causing a bacterial infection, to sling the words at him with her cat's tongue, every syllable covered with a million tiny barbs. They'd snag in the membranes lining his nose, his ears, and fester there. She'd ask him if he knew what his brother had done. He was her last link to his brother, the transparent mucous thread of white when an egg is separated, to the brother who was not there enduring the music, not standing restlessly beneath the lights feeling heat crawl across his skin like a sickening insect, a tick. She wanted them both to know she remembered, she had not forgiven it. Now she stood next to him beside a round table draped in white rayon, laden with a garish centerpiece and trays of meat, flesh sliced so thin she could see through it. And miniature, delicate vegetables were gathered in edible ribbons, in intricate bows and knots, like bouquets in a doll-house. The ballroom is inside the doll-house: the roof's been removed and now she's looking down into it. She doesn't know anyone in there—anyone. And how would he know what his brother had done? How could he know his brother? The next morning she'd tried to pretend it hadn't happened, her pretending becoming the strangest crime of all. No, you did Not, she'd insisted to the brother, receiving him into her body before she never saw him again. To scare them away from cigarettes, her high school had shown the students a film—a human lung was cut into delicate slices, terrifically thin, on a steel machine just like one in a deli. The camera examined a sliver: the lung tissue was elaborate, lacey, crystalline in disease, like the polished plane of a geode. If she sliced the muscle of her heart, would its grain be as simple, as smooth, as these shavings of lox and prosciutto? No, she didn't care for a cocktail. No, not a glass of wine. She wanted silence, ice water. She'd take a swallow, lick and lick and lick and lick the thin flesh of her forearm with her cat's tongue, smoothing the cool damp arm across her flushed face, wiping hair from her eyes, and she'd talk to no one.

Each Day a New Round of Sadness

Islands of the Hawaiian archipelago are connected
to each other under the surface of the sea.

Under the surface of the sea something roils
like a volcano preparing to explode.

To explode sometimes suggests a solution
to the situation of constraint, ubiquitous

as fear these days, when stasis is a prize.
A prize, that is, compared to illness.

Can't wellness sink its teeth deep into me
to feel acutely as a wound?

A wound is what the dream delivers
with an image of my mother

wreathed in Hawaiian flowers—
tuberose releasing its cloying

daylong ennui.

Signs of the Overly Hopeful

Along the Gulf's lousy mirror of wet sand
I run out of anxiety
but it refills me before all the hot water in the shower's gone.

A miserably-married relation said *Every great thing in my life has come
from taking these crazy risks.*

I risk being pessimistic. Even art's becoming disappointing.

In Houston's MFA, galleries of baby-faced Marys, gilt wood
surrounding their patient faces peeling. Joseph's hair is grey
as Jeffrey Epstein's.

Is less rat-racing the answer? Is it obvious as a highway sign?
Brakeless Trucks Must Bypass Rest Area

My friend Lee Anne has a strategy:
*I answer all the officer's questions
with a small amount of truth
and a large amount of practicality.*

A muddle is E. M. Forster's phrase for when we don't know our own minds.

Lee Anne's always known herself: *Calm. But with a twitch.*

Rick said *She has a romantic aversion to the idea of marriage.*

I think sex is the Judas horse that led us into . . . what? the state pen? marriage?
nine years of dust?

Impervious surfaces. Antiquated lamb.

We're older than when we first said these things
but maybe time's on our side?

I want a side of reality. Even when it's grim.

Teens are mad for fantasy because they feel
they have no agency.

In reality we dread Trump could linger past November,
like a rat behind a wall.

I don't want to be overly hopeful
but no one human can accept that smell.

At Galveston Beach, 1935

This is meat, potatoes, & lodging—
Dadda Farrington would say when,
for instance, something irretrievable
was found in wet sand, such as
the coin he'd handed Charlie back
at the house to carry—
Dadda's beer budget—
pilfered from a responsible party &
earmarked for the strand's concessionaire.
Bread of life for some, beer was
the menu for Dadda, transplanted soul
who held the rogue songs of Belfast
till he could lodge them in
the memories of Charlie's children, who
never met the man but through
his appetites, & music.

Memory Fruit

Imagine the jukebox
at the watermelon stand
during the war

or was it a radio playing
Al Martino's tune *You'll Never Know*
(Just How Much I Love You).

My grandmother's tears falling on
her salted melon,
scattered with its own.

If There's a God I'm a Horse's Ass

If I could hope to find you just now
in the flowers, temper and humor me
in crucial hours when stars pulse audibly
(although we call them insects),
when doubts suppressed all day for years
rise to the skies as fireworks,
when I'm as weak as I would ever want to be.
That is, no weaker, please, than this—
O maker, master, electrician, jefe, friend of friends.
Phantom consciousness, to whom I in duress
or bliss address a rare prayer, hedging bets.
Pain in my heart reminds me I will
die sometime, not so very far from now.
Will you be there to shake my hand,
welcome me to heaven as in a *New Yorker* cartoon
where the worst injury's a charley horse,
a flash—acute spasm in the toe or calf
that lasts a minute only?
Why mess with me, only one hair of the hide
on the ass of an animal you made,
and made a fool of.

Spring Fury

Weathers of mind
you descend in violence
through May's
brindled fragrance.
As you come down
I fear my own
force has no border
of minutes or clemency.
Weathers of mind's
space without light
yet electric—
storm-sparked.
On a thousand acres
of estate, only two fields
for the aged:
in one field a single
dead sheep—deflated
desiccated, mud-spackled
fleece flat over grass.
The soul that was
mind months gone.
On the other field
three ancient ewes
—black legs barely
holding over green.
Soul that is the mind
these weathers are
inherited: your only—
your ancestral home.

Spring Poem

for Frances

The Casablanca lilies have fallen apart, only two hardy petals
clinging to a stem. I make tortilla chips back into masa in my mouth
where the last virus bloomed, a virus known and older, in my gums
next to the lower molars, row of worn mortars grinding for life.
Did you say you wanted devolution? Mark it happening here,
every neighbor anxious to cut something down, be it leaves of grass
or weeds or an oak grown overly robust beside electric wires.
Allergic to lilies, you can't be the virgin now, nor I, nor I
though my nose isn't opposed to lilies, twitches only at filaments
of mimosa instigated by wind. Imagine I could go backwards
in experience, subtracting yes from yes until I arrived at my first
kiss, on a Greyhound bus. And though the righteousness of this
location escaped me for years, I savor it now—language sweet
to season loss.

Call It Like You See It

It's plain flat cold.
Dense fog fills the valley below
like crème anglaise.
The Labrador inside his faux fur rug
is Sultan of Dog
and wouldn't say no to a pastry.
Why rise from bed
when the owl yet sings in the mesquite
and no one has made coffee.
Tomorrow without fail
brings rain, more cold.
The Sultan and his retinue
have each grown up and almost
old. Who knows what song
the owl pronounces now
in oval tones—the fable's knell,
or an avian solicitation?

Acknowledgments

Colorado Review, "Cuomo's Important Failures"
Diode Poetry Journal, "Signs of the Overly Hopeful"
Five Points, "Cat's Tongue"
New Ohio Review, "Force of Habit," "Pas de Deux"
Poetry Is Currency, "Crazing"
Processing Crisis Anthology, "Cat's Tongue"

The epigraph by Magdalena Zurawski is from "Eros, Airing Its Burn" in *Companion Animal* (Litmus Press 2015).

Warm thanks to the editors and publications that originally published poems in this chapbook. I'm grateful to everyone at Texas Review Press, and particularly to Director J. Bruce Fuller and Managing Editor PJ Carlisle. Thank you to photographer, "girl-with-red-hat on unsplash" for the amazing cover photo.

Love and gratitude to Greg Campbell, Ray Winter, Frances Townsend Winter, Greg Mahrer, Don Bogen, Eva Valencia, Tom Coffeen, Allison Moseley, Anne Goldman, Francie Salle, John Johnson, Cynthia Hogue, Susan Terris, Cathy Cummins, Jodi Hottel, Zoë Ryder White, Iris Dunkle and the New York Diaspora Poem-a-day Team.

For their artistic support and friendship, many thanks to Michael Adams and the Texas Institute of Letters, Cill Rialaig Project, George David Clark and the *32 Poems* staff, John Nieves, W. Todd Kaneko, David St. John, Katie Berta, Gwen Strauss and the Maison Dora Maar, Nancy White, Ryan Vine, Jennifer Franklin and Michael Shewmaker.